Mama
Akashi
Koala

The Trail Blazer

Margaret Kamla Kumar
Laila Savolainen

U
ma
Publishing
Group

A catalogue record for this book is available from the National Library of Australia

ISBN: 978-0-6454789-8-3 (hardback)
ISBN: 978-0-6454789-6-9 (paperback)
ISBN 978-0-6454789-7-6 (ebook)

This book is part of the: Kashy Koala Series
Author: Margaret Kamla Kumar
Illustrator: Laila Savolainen

Interior / Cover / Artwork: Pickawoowoo Author Services
Print and Channel Distribution: Lightning Source / Ingram (US/UK/AUS/ EUR)

Publisher: Uma Publishing Group
www.umapublishing.com

Dedication

This book is dedicated to the continuing partnership between humankind and the flora and fauna of the physical environment.

Mama Akashi Koala was feeling nervous. She could sense something in the wind. Her nose was telling her so because it was beginning to twitch in a particular way. She began to look around.

At the same time, she began reaching down into her pouch to see that Koalakin, her joey, was safe.

"Look yonder," Mama Akashi Koala called out to Grandfather Kashy Koala. "Do you see what I see?"

Grandfather Kashy Koala opened his sleepy eyes and peered into the distance. "No, I don't. What do you see?"

Mama Akashi Koala repeated her question. She then said, "Can't you see the orange lights rushing into the sky? It looks like the sun is rising in the middle of the night."

"Ohhhhhhhh!" said Kashy Koala in consternation, "They are flames. There must be a bushfire in the distance. Hopefully, they won't come our way?"

Sure enough, the wind changed, and the fire disappeared into the distance. But Mama Akashi Koala was still feeling nervous. Something was not right. The fires indicated that there were more things to come.

The next day her fears were confirmed. Some humans arrived with equipment while the koalas were still sleeping.

Mama Akashi saw and sensed that from the koala world's point of view, the humans were here to cut down trees and destroy their homes.

She knew that the humans must have their reasons for doing so but this was their space too.

"I don't think the humans are aware of this," she surmised.

Mama Akashi decided that some sort of action was needed to stop the destruction of their home, their environment, and their food source.

She began to make koala sounds to attract the attention of her koala colony.

The koalas woke up to the sound of Mama Akashi's bellowing, grunts, and shrill noises.

They knew that something was not right. Otherwise, Mama Akashi would not disturb them.

So, they began walking and climbing to Mama Akashi's tree home.

"See what is happening," Mama Akashi said to the group, indicating the humans coming toward them with their machinery.

"They are going to take away our land and livelihood again as they did at our previous place.

We need to do something.

We need to act fast.

If not, we are going to become a lost cause like all our other animal friends who have disappeared from this land."

The other koalas were dumbstruck. This was the first time someone from their own koala colony had spoken to them in this way. And that too in a long speech. They were always known to be shy and quiet.

Even Grandfather Kashy just stood and stared.

Eventually, one of the members of the koala colony spoke up. "Well, what do you want us to do?"

"The first thing we need to do is stand up for ourselves," Mama Akashi said. "We haven't found a word for it yet in our *koalaspeak* language because we have not done this before. But we shall do it through action. We are going to stand together side by side and not move as the humans come closer and closer with their gigantic machinery."

And that is exactly what the colony of koalas did!

It was a sight to behold! The whole koala colony was lined up, side by side. The workers were puzzled by this action. They had never seen this before. No one from the animal world had done this to them before.

The workers said shocked, "What are they doing?"

Mama Akashi with Grandfather Kashy Koala and the older koalas stood there quietly, not moving an inch. They were showing a quiet resistance that took the humans by surprise. The workers decided to stop for the day and leave the koalas' space.

"They will be back as night follows day," Mama Akashi told the colony of koalas. "And we shall be here again, won't we?"

"Of course, we shall," they replied in one voice.

"Wonderful. We won't be finished until they know that this space is to be shared by all of us, animals and humans alike," Mama Akashi said.

The next day, the koala colony assembled again before the workers arrived.

This time, Mama Akashi got all the little koalas together with Koalakin and put them next to the older koalas.

"Would you like to do something to save our home, our habitat?" she asked them.

"Is it fun?" one of the younger members of the group said.

"Not really," Mama Akashi said. "But it sends out an important message."

"Of course," another member of the group said.

"That means we are *important* too."

Seeing how enthusiastic they were, Mama Akashi got all of them to hold eucalyptus leaves in their mouths to show the humans that the leaves of the eucalyptus trees were their food for survival.

The workers arrived the next day. This time seeing the colony of koalas, standing there with the eucalyptus leaves in their mouths made them feel embarrassed.

After standing around for hours, they decided to pack up but left their equipment behind. 'We'll be back, tomorrow," one of them yelled out.

"Of course, you will," Mama Akashi called out in a bellow. "And we shall be waiting."

Mama Akashi collected the koala group again and pepped them up by saying, "We koalas are strong. Look at our claws. They are sharp and help us to climb trees. The two thumbs on our forepaws give us a good grip for climbing trees."

"Tomorrow before the humans arrive, each one of us with our families will climb halfway up the eucalyptus tree that we call our home and stay there. When the workers arrive, they will see each of us holding on to our home. What do you think?"

"Fantastic idea. Let's do it," all of them said.

The next day when the workers arrived, they saw groups of koalas clinging halfway up around each of the eucalyptus trees. All they could do was stand and shake their heads.

Suddenly, their supervisor stepped forward, looked at the koalas on the trees, and said, "We get the message, koala friends. We know that this is your home. We are leaving." With that, the supervisor told his team to gather up their equipment and tools and leave the area.

Mama Akashi looked back at the supervisor and nodded her thanks. He had understood their needs.

After they left, Mama Akashi called out to everyone. "Come on everyone, we have taken the first step. Let's move ahead and protect our home and environment."

The koala colony nodded in agreement with bellows, grunts, and shrills.

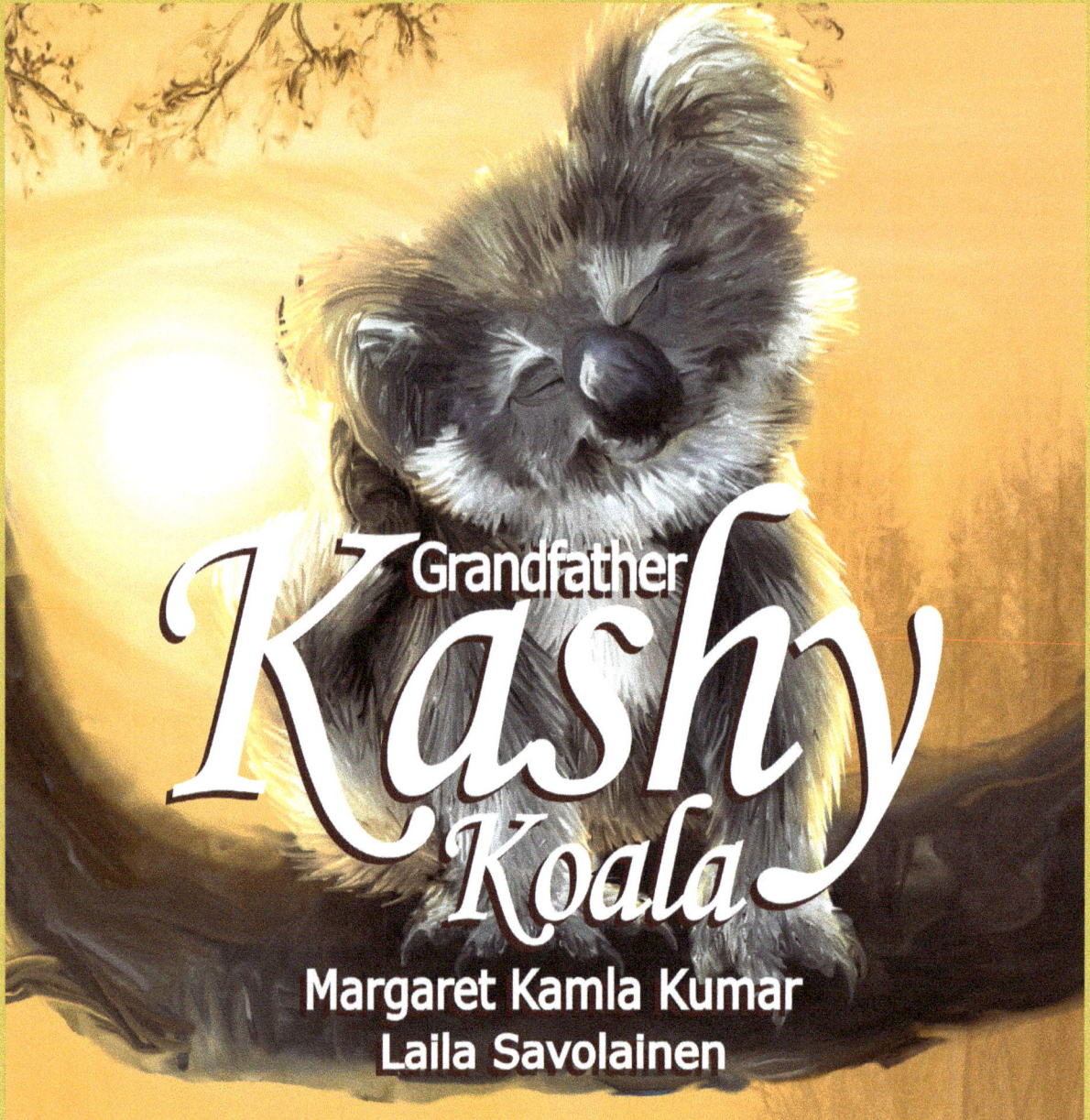

Grandfather
Kashy
Koala

Margaret Kamla Kumar
Laila Savolainen

Young Joey Koalakin

Margaret Kamla Kumar

Laila Savolainen

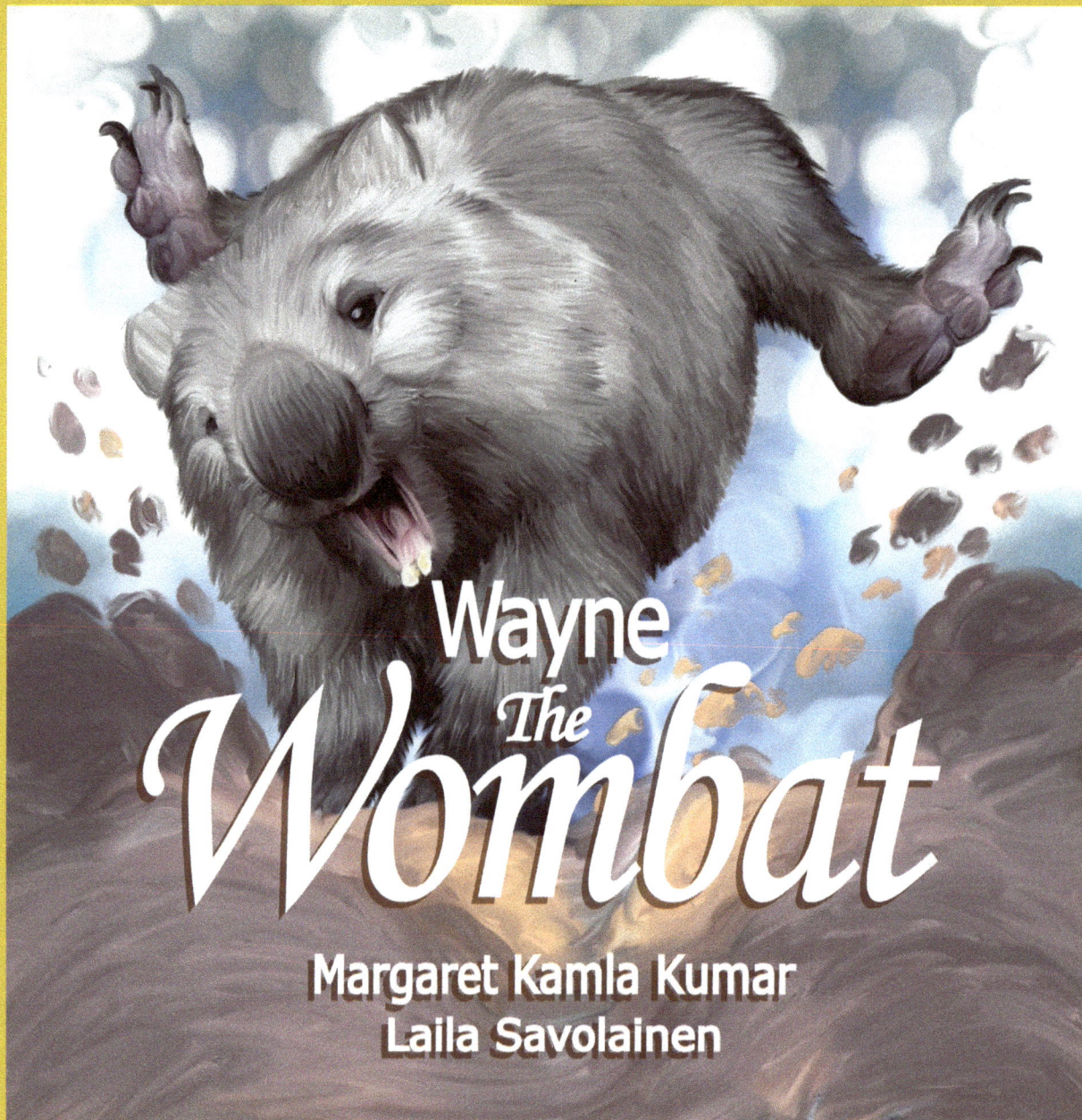

Wayne
The
Wombat

Margaret Kamla Kumar
Laila Savolainen

www.ingramcontent.com/pod-product-compliance
Lightning Source LLC
Chambersburg PA
CBHW051557030426
42334CB00034B/3473